STEALING YOUR MANDATE

The Build up to 2023 Nigeria General Elections

Isaac William

Table of Contents

Conclusion

Introduction

The 2023 Nigeria General Election was a critical milestone in the country's democratic journey. As the nation prepared to elect its leaders, there was a growing concern about the potential for mandate theft and the erosion of democratic principles. This book, "Stealing Your Mandate in relation to 2023 Nigeria Election," delves into the complex issue of mandate theft and its impact on Nigeria's political landscape.

Chapter 1 provides an introduction to the 2023 Nigeria Election, highlighting its significance in shaping the country's future. It offers a brief overview of the mandate and its importance in the electoral process.

Chapter 2 delves into the concept of a mandate, defining its meaning and exploring its significance in politics. It examines the power and responsibility associated with a mandate and how it can be used to drive positive change.

Chapter 3 takes a historical perspective, analyzing past instances of mandate theft in Nigerian elections. By examining patterns and common strategies employed, readers gain a deeper understanding of the complexities surrounding this issue.

Chapter 4 explores the factors contributing to mandate theft, including political, social, and economic influences. It also addresses the role of corruption and electoral malpractices in enabling mandate theft.

In Chapter 5, readers are presented with case studies of mandate theft in recent Nigerian elections. These real-life examples shed light on the impact of mandate theft on democracy, governance, and public trust.

Chapter 6 delves into the consequences of mandate theft, highlighting the far-reaching repercussions on Nigerian society. It explores the implications for democracy, governance, and the overall well-being of the nation.

Chapter 7 focuses on strategies for preventing mandate theft, offering potential solutions and measures to safeguard the electoral process. It emphasizes the importance of strengthening institutions and promoting transparency.

The role of civil society organizations and the international community is examined in Chapter 8. It highlights the significance of their involvement in preventing mandate theft and supporting free and fair elections.

Chapter 9 emphasizes the importance of citizen action and advocacy in combating mandate theft. It provides strategies for mobilizing public support and empowering citizens to actively participate in the electoral process.

In Chapter 10, the book looks ahead to the future, providing recommendations for electoral reforms and improvements. It emphasizes the need to build a resilient democracy and protect the mandate of the people.

The appendix includes a list of resources and references for further reading, including relevant books, articles, reports, websites, and organizations working on electoral integrity in Nigeria.

This book aims to shed light on the issue of mandate theft in relation to the 2023 Nigeria Election. By exploring its causes, consequences, and potential solutions, it seeks to empower readers with knowledge and inspire action towards ensuring free and fair elections in Nigeria.

CHAPTER ONE
The Mandate

The mandate is a concept that holds great significance in the political landscape of any nation, including Nigeria. In the context of elections, a mandate refers to the authority and power given to a candidate or political party by the electorate to govern and make decisions on their behalf. It is a form of social contract between the elected representatives and the people, where the elected officials are entrusted with the responsibility to fulfill the promises made during the election campaign.

The mandate is not merely a symbolic gesture; it carries immense weight and implications for the governance and development of a country. It represents the will of the people and serves as a guiding principle for the elected officials to shape policies and make decisions that align with the aspirations and needs of the electorate.

The significance of the mandate lies in its ability to legitimize the authority of the elected government. When a candidate or party secures a majority of votes or seats in an election, it is seen as a validation of their policies, ideologies, and leadership qualities. The mandate bestows upon them the power to implement their agenda and enact reforms that they believe will benefit the nation.

Furthermore, the mandate serves as a mechanism of accountability. Elected officials are expected to fulfill their electoral promises and work towards the betterment of society. The mandate empowers the people to hold their representatives accountable for their actions and decisions. If elected officials fail to deliver on their promises or act against the interests of the people, they risk losing their mandate in subsequent elections.

However, the significance of the mandate can be undermined when mandate theft occurs. Mandate theft refers to the manipulation or distortion of election results through fraudulent practices, such as rigging, vote-buying, or intimidation. When the true will of the people is subverted, the legitimacy of the elected government is compromised, and the mandate loses its meaning.

To safeguard the integrity of the mandate, it is crucial to ensure free and fair elections, strengthen democratic institutions, and promote transparency and accountability in the electoral process. This requires the active participation of citizens, civil society organizations, and the international community in monitoring and advocating for electoral integrity.

In conclusion, the mandate is a fundamental concept in politics that defines the authority and responsibility of elected officials. Its significance lies in its ability to legitimize the government's authority, hold elected representatives accountable, and shape the direction of a nation. Protecting and preserving the mandate is essential for upholding democratic principles and ensuring good governance in Nigeria.

CHAPTER TWO
Historical Analysis of Mandate Theft in Nigerian Elections

Mandate theft, the manipulation or distortion of election results, has been a recurring issue in Nigerian elections throughout history. A historical analysis of mandate theft provides valuable insights into the patterns, strategies, and consequences of this phenomenon.

Nigeria's electoral history is marred by instances of mandate theft, where the true will of the people is subverted through various fraudulent practices. These practices include rigging, ballot box stuffing, voter intimidation, and vote-buying. Mandate theft often involves collusion between political actors, electoral officials, and security personnel, creating a complex web of corruption and manipulation.

One of the earliest instances of mandate theft in Nigeria can be traced back to the First Republic in the 1960s. The political landscape was characterized by intense competition between regional parties, leading to widespread electoral fraud. Mandate theft was used as a means to consolidate power and maintain dominance in the regions. This pattern continued in subsequent elections, with mandate theft becoming increasingly sophisticated and pervasive.

The Second Republic, which lasted from 1979 to 1983, witnessed a similar trend of mandate theft. Political parties resorted to various tactics to manipulate election outcomes, including ballot box snatching, falsification of results, and violence. Mandate theft during this period contributed to the erosion of public trust in the electoral process and the eventual collapse of the Second Republic.

The return to democratic rule in 1999 brought renewed hope for free and fair elections in Nigeria. However, mandate theft persisted, albeit in different forms. The use of technology, such as voter card cloning and manipulation of electronic voting systems, added new dimensions to mandate theft. Additionally, the influence of money and the use of political thugs became more prevalent, further undermining the integrity of the electoral process.

The consequences of mandate theft are far-reaching. It undermines the legitimacy of elected governments, erodes public trust in democracy, and perpetuates a cycle of corruption and impunity. Mandate theft also exacerbates social and political tensions, leading to instability and potential violence.

To address the issue of mandate theft, it is crucial to learn from historical patterns and develop strategies to prevent and combat this phenomenon. Strengthening electoral institutions, enhancing transparency and accountability, and promoting civic education are essential steps in safeguarding the integrity of elections.

In conclusion, a historical analysis of mandate theft in Nigerian elections reveals a troubling pattern of corruption and manipulation. Understanding the strategies employed and the consequences of mandate theft is crucial in developing effective measures to ensure free and fair elections in Nigeria. By learning from the past, Nigeria can strive to build a more inclusive and democratic society.

CHAPTER THREE
Factors Contributing to Mandate Theft

Mandate theft is a serious issue that affects individuals and organizations alike. It refers to the unauthorized acquisition or misuse of someone's power or authority to carry out certain tasks or make decisions. The consequences of mandate theft can be far-reaching, leading to financial loss, reputational damage, and legal implications. Understanding the factors that contribute to mandate theft is crucial in preventing and mitigating this type of fraud.

One of the primary factors contributing to mandate theft is the lack of proper internal controls within organizations. When there is a lack of oversight and accountability, individuals with access to sensitive information and decision-making power can easily exploit their positions for personal gain. This can include manipulating financial transactions, misappropriating funds, or making unauthorized decisions on behalf of the organization.

Another factor that contributes to mandate theft is the presence of weak or outdated technology systems. In today's digital age, cybercriminals are constantly evolving their tactics to exploit vulnerabilities in computer networks and software. Organizations that fail to invest in robust cybersecurity measures are at a higher risk of falling victim to mandate theft. This can include phishing attacks, malware injections, or hacking into systems to gain unauthorized access to sensitive information.

Furthermore, inadequate employee training and awareness play a significant role in mandate theft. Employees who are not properly educated on the risks and consequences of mandate theft may unknowingly engage in fraudulent activities or become susceptible to manipulation by external parties. Therefore, organizations must invest in ongoing training programs to ensure that their employees are equipped with the knowledge and skills to identify and report suspicious activities.

Additionally, a lack of ethical culture within organizations can contribute to mandate theft. When there is a culture that tolerates unethical behavior or turns a blind eye to suspicious activities, individuals may feel more inclined to engage in fraudulent acts. Organizations must foster a culture of integrity, where employees are encouraged to report any wrongdoing without fear of retaliation.

In conclusion, mandate theft is a serious issue that requires proactive measures to prevent and mitigate its occurrence. Factors such as the lack of internal controls, weak technology systems, inadequate employee training, and an unethical culture contribute to the vulnerability of organizations to mandate theft. By addressing these factors and implementing robust internal controls, organizations can significantly reduce the risk of mandate theft and protect their assets and reputation.

CHAPTER FOUR
Case Studies: Mandate Theft in Recent Nigeria Elections

Mandate theft is a grave concern in electoral processes, as it undermines the democratic principles of fair and transparent elections. In recent years, Nigeria has experienced several cases of mandate theft, raising concerns about the integrity of the electoral system. This article will examine some notable case studies of mandate theft in recent Nigeria elections.

One prominent case of mandate theft occurred during the 2019 general elections in Nigeria. In the state of Rivers, there were reports of widespread violence, voter intimidation, and ballot box snatching. These acts of violence and intimidation were aimed at suppressing voter turnout and manipulating the election results in favor of certain candidates. The Independent National Electoral Commission (INEC) had to suspend the elections in some areas due to the security risks posed by these incidents.

Another case study of mandate theft took place during the 2015 gubernatorial elections in Kogi State. In this instance, there were allegations of electoral malpractice, including the manipulation of voter registration lists and the use of violence to intimidate voters. The election was marred by reports of ballot box snatching, multiple voting, and falsification of results. These actions undermined the credibility of the electoral process and raised concerns about the legitimacy of the elected officials.

Furthermore, the 2011 presidential elections in Nigeria witnessed several cases of mandate theft. In some areas, there were reports of ballot stuffing, voter suppression, and tampering with election results. These fraudulent activities were aimed at manipulating the outcome of the elections and ensuring the victory of certain candidates. The widespread nature of these incidents highlighted the need for stronger measures to prevent and address mandate theft in Nigeria.

The prevalence of mandate theft in recent Nigeria elections can be attributed to various factors. These include the lack of adequate security measures, weak enforcement of electoral laws, and the influence of money and power in politics. Additionally, the lack of awareness and education among voters about their rights and the electoral process makes them more susceptible to manipulation and coercion.

To address the issue of mandate theft in Nigeria, it is crucial to strengthen the institutions responsible for organizing and overseeing elections. This includes enhancing the capacity of the INEC, improving security measures, and ensuring the impartiality and independence of electoral officials. Additionally, there is a need for increased civic education and awareness campaigns to empower voters and reduce their vulnerability to manipulation.

In conclusion, mandate theft remains a significant challenge in Nigeria's electoral system. The case studies mentioned above highlight the various forms of electoral malpractice and fraud that have occurred in recent elections. To uphold the principles of democracy and ensure free and fair elections, it is essential for Nigeria to address the factors contributing to mandate theft and implement measures to prevent and punish those involved in such acts.

CHAPTER FIVE
The consequences of mandate theft

Mandate theft, the unauthorized acquisition or misuse of someone's power or authority, can have severe consequences for individuals and organizations alike. The impact of mandate theft can range from financial loss and reputational damage to legal implications and erosion of trust. Understanding the consequences of mandate theft is crucial in highlighting the importance of preventing and addressing this type of fraud.

One of the primary consequences of mandate theft is financial loss. When individuals or organizations fall victim to mandate theft, they can experience significant monetary damage. This can include misappropriation of funds, fraudulent financial transactions, or unauthorized use of resources. The financial repercussions can be particularly devastating for smaller organizations or individuals who may not have the resources to recover from such losses.

Reputational damage is another significant consequence of mandate theft. When an organization or individual's authority is misused or exploited, it can tarnish their reputation and credibility. This can lead to a loss of trust and confidence from stakeholders, including clients, customers, and partners. Rebuilding a damaged reputation can be a challenging and time-consuming process, impacting future business opportunities and relationships.

Mandate theft can also have legal implications. Depending on the nature and scale of the theft, it may be considered a criminal offense. Legal consequences can include fines, imprisonment, or other penalties. Additionally, individuals or organizations may face civil lawsuits from affected parties seeking restitution for the damages incurred.

Another consequence of mandate theft is the erosion of trust in institutions and the democratic process. When individuals or organizations abuse their authority, it undermines the principles of transparency, fairness, and accountability. This can lead to a loss of faith in the electoral system, government institutions, or other organizations. Restoring trust and confidence in these institutions can be a long and challenging process, requiring significant reforms and measures to prevent future mandate theft.

In conclusion, the consequences of mandate theft are far-reaching and can have severe implications for individuals and organizations. Financial loss, reputational damage, legal consequences, and erosion of trust are among the significant impacts of mandate theft. It is crucial for individuals, organizations, and governments to prioritize prevention, detection, and prosecution of mandate theft to safeguard against these consequences and uphold the principles of integrity and accountability.

CHAPTER SIX
Strategies for Preventing Mandate Theft

Preventing mandate theft, the unauthorized acquisition or misuse of someone's power or authority, requires proactive measures and robust internal controls. By implementing the following strategies, individuals and organizations can significantly reduce the risk of mandate theft and protect their assets and reputation.

Firstly, establishing strong internal controls is crucial in preventing mandate theft. This includes implementing segregation of duties, where no single individual has complete control over a process or decision. By separating responsibilities, organizations can reduce the risk of collusion and unauthorized actions. Additionally, regular monitoring and auditing of financial transactions and decision-making processes can help detect any suspicious activities or deviations from established procedures.

Secondly, investing in robust technology systems and cybersecurity measures is essential. Organizations should ensure that their computer networks, software, and data storage systems are secure and regularly updated. This includes implementing firewalls, encryption, and multi-factor authentication to protect against unauthorized access and data breaches. Regular cybersecurity training for employees is also vital in raising awareness about the risks of mandate theft and how to recognize and report suspicious activities.

Thirdly, promoting a culture of integrity and ethics within organizations is crucial in preventing mandate theft. This includes establishing a code of conduct that clearly outlines expected behavior and consequences for non-compliance.

Organizations should encourage employees to report any suspicious activities or concerns without fear of retaliation. By fostering an environment where honesty and accountability are valued, individuals are less likely to engage in fraudulent acts.

Furthermore, conducting thorough background checks and vetting processes for individuals in positions of authority is essential. Organizations should verify the credentials and qualifications of potential employees or partners before granting them access to sensitive information or decision-making power. This can help prevent individuals with a history of fraudulent behavior or unethical conduct from assuming positions where they can exploit their authority.

Lastly, ongoing training and education programs for employees are crucial in preventing mandate theft. These programs should focus on raising awareness about the risks and consequences of mandate theft, as well as providing employees with the knowledge and skills to identify and report suspicious activities. By empowering employees to be vigilant and proactive, organizations can create a strong line of defense against mandate theft.

In conclusion, preventing mandate theft requires a multi-faceted approach that includes strong internal controls, robust technology systems, an ethical culture, thorough vetting processes, and ongoing training programs. By implementing these strategies, individuals and organizations can significantly reduce the risk of mandate theft and protect their interests and reputation.

CHAPTER SEVEN
The Role of Civil Society and International Community in Preventing Mandate Theft

Mandate theft, also known as electoral fraud or election rigging, is a significant threat to democracy and good governance. It undermines the will of the people and erodes trust in the electoral process. To combat this menace, the role of civil society and the international community is crucial in preventing mandate theft and ensuring free and fair elections.

Civil society organizations (CSOs) play a vital role in monitoring and safeguarding the electoral process. They act as watchdogs, ensuring that elections are conducted in a transparent and accountable manner. CSOs can engage in various activities such as voter education, election observation, and advocacy for electoral reforms. By actively participating in these activities, civil society can raise awareness among citizens about their rights and responsibilities in the electoral process. This empowers individuals to make informed choices and reduces the likelihood of mandate theft.

Furthermore, CSOs can monitor the entire electoral cycle, from voter registration to the announcement of results. They can observe polling stations, scrutinize ballot counting processes, and report any irregularities or malpractices. This monitoring helps to deter potential perpetrators of mandate theft and provides evidence for legal action if necessary. Additionally, CSOs can work closely with electoral management bodies to ensure that they are independent, impartial, and adequately resourced to conduct elections effectively.

The international community also plays a critical role in preventing mandate theft. International organizations, such as the United Nations and regional bodies like the African Union and the Organization of American States, can provide technical assistance and support to countries in strengthening their electoral systems. This includes capacity building for electoral management bodies, training for election observers, and support for electoral reforms. The presence of international observers during elections can serve as a deterrent to mandate theft and provide an impartial assessment of the electoral process.

Moreover, the international community can exert diplomatic pressure on countries where mandate theft is suspected or detected. By condemning such actions and imposing targeted sanctions, they can send a strong message that electoral fraud will not be tolerated. This can help to create a conducive environment for free and fair elections and encourage governments to uphold democratic principles.

In conclusion, preventing mandate theft requires a multi-faceted approach involving both civil society and the international community. CSOs play a crucial role in monitoring the electoral process and empowering citizens, while the international community provides technical assistance, support, and diplomatic pressure. By working together, they can help ensure that the will of the people is respected, and democratic governance is upheld.

CHAPTER EIGHT
Mobilizing for Change:
Citizen Action and Advocacy

Citizen action and advocacy are powerful tools for driving social and political change. When individuals come together to voice their concerns, demand accountability, and advocate for their rights, they can create a significant impact on society. Mobilizing for change through citizen action and advocacy is essential for promoting democracy, social justice, and sustainable development.

Citizen action involves individuals actively participating in civic activities to address issues that affect their lives and communities. It can take various forms, such as protests, demonstrations, petitions, and grassroots organizing. By mobilizing and uniting their voices, citizens can bring attention to pressing issues and put pressure on decision-makers to take action.

Advocacy, on the other hand, focuses on influencing policies and decisions through strategic communication and engagement with policymakers. Advocates work to raise awareness, build public support, and influence public opinion to bring about change. They gather evidence, conduct research, and develop persuasive arguments to make a compelling case for policy reforms or changes in practices.

One of the key advantages of citizen action and advocacy is that they give a voice to marginalized and underrepresented groups. By organizing and advocating for their rights, these groups can challenge systemic inequalities and demand equal opportunities and access to resources. Citizen action and advocacy also empower individuals to take ownership of their communities and actively participate in decision-making processes.

Furthermore, citizen action and advocacy can hold governments and institutions accountable for their actions or lack thereof. By monitoring the implementation of policies and programs, citizens can ensure that their demands are met and that public resources are used effectively and transparently. This helps to prevent corruption, mismanagement, and abuse of power.

In recent years, citizen action and advocacy have played a crucial role in addressing various global challenges, such as climate change, gender inequality, and human rights abuses. Movements like Fridays for Future, #MeToo, and Black Lives Matter have shown the power of collective action in shaping public discourse and driving policy changes.

In conclusion, mobilizing for change through citizen action and advocacy is instrumental in promoting social justice, democracy, and sustainable development. By coming together, citizens can amplify their voices, demand accountability, and advocate for their rights. In an increasingly interconnected world, citizen action and advocacy are essential for creating a more inclusive, just, and equitable society.

CHAPTER NINE
Looking Ahead: Ensuring Free and Fair Elections in Nigeria in 2027

Free and fair elections are the cornerstone of any democratic society. In Nigeria, the upcoming elections in 2027 present an opportunity to strengthen the country's democratic institutions and ensure that the will of the people is respected. However, several challenges need to be addressed to ensure that the elections are conducted in a transparent and accountable manner.

One of the key challenges is the issue of electoral violence and insecurity. In the past, Nigeria has experienced instances of violence and intimidation during elections, which undermines the integrity of the process and discourages citizens from participating. To address this, it is crucial for the government to prioritize the security of voters, candidates, and election officials. Adequate measures should be put in place to prevent and respond to any form of violence or intimidation, and those responsible should be held accountable.

Another challenge is the need for electoral reforms to enhance the credibility of the electoral process. Nigeria has made progress in this regard with the passage of the Electoral Act Amendment Bill in 2018. However, there is still room for improvement. It is important for the government and relevant stakeholders to continue working towards implementing the necessary reforms, such as the use of technology in voter registration and result collation, to reduce the chances of manipulation and ensure the accuracy and transparency of the electoral process.

Furthermore, ensuring a level playing field for all candidates is essential for free and fair elections. This includes guaranteeing equal access to media coverage, campaign financing regulations, and creating an environment that allows for peaceful and constructive political competition. The government and electoral management bodies should work closely with civil society organizations, the media, and other stakeholders to promote fairness and impartiality throughout the electoral process.

Additionally, voter education and civic engagement are vital in ensuring informed participation and reducing voter apathy. Efforts should be made to educate citizens about their rights and responsibilities in the electoral process, as well as the importance of their vote in shaping the future of the country. This can be done through public awareness campaigns, community dialogues, and the use of social media platforms to reach a wider audience.

In conclusion, ensuring free and fair elections in Nigeria in 2027 requires addressing challenges such as electoral violence, electoral reforms, creating a level playing field, and promoting voter education and civic engagement. By taking proactive measures to tackle these issues, Nigeria can strengthen its democratic institutions and build public trust in the electoral process. This will contribute to the consolidation of democracy and the overall development of the country.

Conclusion

"Stealing Your Mandate: A Wake-Up Call for the 2027 Nigeria Election"

The book "Stealing Your Mandate" serves as a powerful wake-up call for the upcoming 2027 Nigeria Election. It sheds light on the pressing issue of mandate theft and its implications for democracy and good governance in Nigeria. The author's insightful analysis and compelling narratives bring to the forefront the challenges faced by the Nigerian electoral system and the urgent need for reform.

The book highlights the importance of free and fair elections as the cornerstone of democracy. It emphasizes that the will of the people must be respected, and their votes should not be manipulated or stolen. The author delves into the various tactics employed by perpetrators of mandate theft, such as voter intimidation, ballot stuffing, and result manipulation. By exposing these tactics, the book aims to raise awareness and mobilize citizens to actively participate in safeguarding the integrity of the electoral process.

Moreover, "Stealing Your Mandate" provides a comprehensive overview of the factors contributing to mandate theft in Nigeria. It examines the role of political actors, electoral management bodies, and the security apparatus in perpetuating or preventing electoral fraud. The book underscores the need for accountability and transparency at all levels of the electoral system to ensure that the will of the people prevails.

The author also offers practical solutions and recommendations for preventing mandate theft in the 2027 Nigeria Election. These include strengthening electoral laws, enhancing the independence and capacity of electoral management bodies, and promoting civic education and engagement. The book emphasizes the importance of citizen action and advocacy in holding government officials accountable and demanding electoral reforms.

In conclusion, "Stealing Your Mandate" serves as a timely and thought-provoking resource for all stakeholders involved in the 2027 Nigeria Election. It highlights the critical importance of free and fair elections and the need to address the challenges of mandate theft. By heeding the wake-up call presented in this book, Nigeria can take significant steps towards strengthening its democratic institutions, restoring public trust, and ensuring that the will of the people is respected in the upcoming election and beyond.

www.ingramcontent.com/pod-product-compliance
Lightning Source LLC
Chambersburg PA
CBHW071006260726
48661CB00007B/2812